# English Foundation Plus

# Activity Book B

Published by Collins
An imprint of HarperCollins*Publishers*
The News Building, 1 London Bridge Street,
London, SE1 9GF, UK

HarperCollins*Publishers*
Macken House, 39/40 Mayor Street Upper,
Dublin 1, DO1 C9W8, Ireland

Browse the complete Collins catalogue at
www.collins.co.uk

10 9 8 7 6 5 4 3

ISBN 978-0-00-846861-3

British Library Cataloguing-in-Publication Data
A catalogue record for this publication is available from the British Library.

Author: Fiona Macgregor
Publisher: Elaine Higgleton
Product manager: Letitia Luff
Commissioning editor: Rachel Houghton
Edited by: Hannah Hirst-Dunton
Editorial management: Oriel Square
Cover designer: Kevin Robbins
Cover illustrations: Jouve India Pvt. Ltd.
Internal illustrations: Jouve India Pvt. Ltd.,
p 2–6 Gustavo Mazili, p 7–10 Parwinder Singh,
p 16–18 Gwyneth Williamson
Typesetter: Jouve India Pvt. Ltd.
Production controller: Lyndsey Rogers
Printed and bound in the UK using 100% Renewable
Electricity at Martins the Printers

Acknowledgements

With thanks to all the kindergarten staff and their schools around the world who
have helped with the development of this course, by sharing insights and
commenting on and testing sample materials:

Calcutta International School: Sharmila Majumdar, Mrs Pratima Nayar, Preeti
Roychoudhury, Tinku Yadav, Lakshmi Khanna, Mousumi Guha, Radhika Dhanuka,
Archana Tiwari, Urmita Das; Gateway College (Sri Lanka): Kousala Benedict; Hawar
International School: Kareen Barakat, Shahla Mohammed, Jennah Hussain; Manthan
International School: Shalini Reddy; Monterey Pre-Primary: Adina Oram; Prometheus
School: Aneesha Sahni, Deepa Nanda; Pragyanam School: Monika Sachdev; Rosary
Sisters High School: Samar Sabat, Sireen Freij, Hiba Mousa; Solitaire Global School:
Devi Nimmagadda; United Charter Schools (UCS): Tabassum Murtaza and
staff; Vietnam Australia International School: Holly Simpson

The publishers gratefully acknowledge the permission granted to reproduce the
copyright material in this book. Every effort has been made to trace copyright
holders and to obtain their permission for the use of copyright material. The
publishers will gladly receive any information enabling them to rectify any
error or omission at the first opportunity.

Extracts from Collins Big Cat readers reprinted by permission of
HarperCollins*Publishers* Ltd

All © HarperCollins*Publishers*

MIX
Paper | Supporting
responsible forestry
FSC™ C007454

This book is produced from independently
certified FSC™ paper to ensure responsible
forest management.

For more information visit:
www.harpercollins.co.uk/green

# Draw

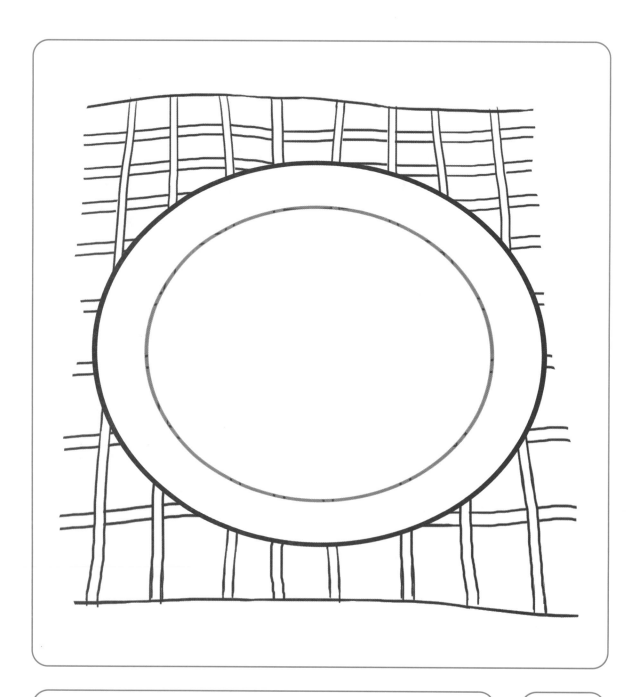

What is your favourite picnic food?
Draw it on the plate.

Date:

# Match

rug

wasps

drinks

cakes

basket

Draw a line to match each word to its picture.

Date:

# Find

Help the family to find their picnic basket.

Date:

# Colour

1 = yellow   2 = red   3 = purple   4 = brown

Follow the number code to finish the picture.

Date:

# Trace and say

cakes

Trace the letter. Say the sound.
Say the word.

Date:

# Put in order

## 1 2 3 4

What happened to make Finn feel better? Number the pictures to match the order of the story.     Date:

# Circle and draw

What would you put in the box, if you were moving home? Circle the things. Draw your own things too.   Date:

# Trace and say

I am sad

| Trace the letters. Say the sentence. |  |
|---|---|
| Date: |  |

# Draw

Draw something that has made you feel
happy today.

Date:

# Trace and say

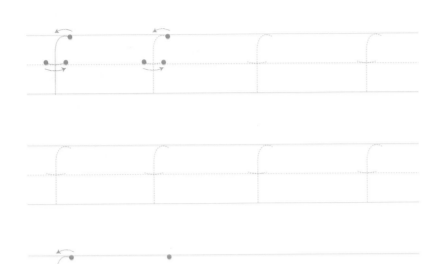

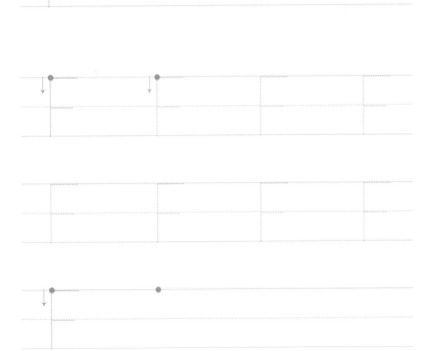

Finn

Trace the letter. Say the sound. Say the word.

Date:

# Find and circle

    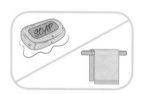

Follow the pattern in each line.
Circle what comes next.

Date:

# Circle

Circle all the things that start with the 'w' sound.

Date:

# Follow

Trace over the dotted lines from each boat
to the end of the page.

Date:

# Trace and say

**water**

Trace the letter. Say the sound.
Say the word.

Date:

# Put in order

**1**  **2**  **3**  **4**

Number the pictures to match the order
of the story.

Date:

# Match

park

beach

woods

home

Match the words to the pictures.

Date:

# Find

Help the girl to find her way home.

Date:

# Trace and say

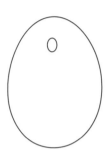

egg

Trace the letter. Say the sound. Say the word.

Date:

# Match

home time

school time

wake-up time

bed time

Match the words to the pictures.

Date:

# Draw

The best time

What do you think is the best time of day? Draw what
you do at that time. Trace the letters. Say the words.    Date:

# Alphabet time

ink

jug   kitten

lemon

mug

Alongside structured phonics lessons, you may want to display and talk about one letter of the alphabet in an 'alphabet time' session each week.

# Alphabet time

nut

octopus

pear

queen

Alongside structured phonics lessons, you may want to display and talk about one letter of the alphabet in an 'alphabet time' session each week.

# Assessment record

_____ has achieved these English Foundation Plus Objectives:

## Reading

| | | | |
|---|---|---|---|
| R1 Develop an increasing awareness of sound structures in language | 1 | 2 | 3 |
| R2 Consolidate and develop early reading skills | 1 | 2 | 3 |
| R3 Recognise more letters of the English alphabet, and their corresponding sounds | 1 | 2 | 3 |
| R4 Begin to use phonemes to read single-syllable words with short vowels | 1 | 2 | 3 |
| Reading motor skills | 1 | 2 | 3 |

## Writing

| | | | |
|---|---|---|---|
| W1 Consolidate early writing skills | 1 | 2 | 3 |
| Writing motor skills | 1 | 2 | 3 |

## Speaking

| | | | |
|---|---|---|---|
| S1 Be able to express oneself in a range of everyday situations | 1 | 2 | 3 |
| S2 Sentences and words: begin to segment and blend | 1 | 2 | 3 |
| Speaking developmental skills | 1 | 2 | 3 |

## Listening

| | | | |
|---|---|---|---|
| L1 Know how to listen and respond appropriately in a range of everyday contexts | 1 | 2 | 3 |
| Listening developmental skills | 1 | 2 | 3 |

1: Partially achieved
2: Achieved
3: Exceeded

Signed by teacher:
Signed by parent:                    Date: